CONURES

EVERYTHING YOU NEED TO KNOW ABOUT CONURES AND ITS CARE GUIDE

RICHARD JAMES

Table of Contents

CHAPTER ONE 4
    INTRODUCTION 4
    THEY LOVE TO PLAY 6
    THEY ARE SMART 7
CHAPTER TWO 8
    REASONS CONURES MAKE GREAT FAMILY PETS 8
    1. ADAPTABLE AND RESILIENT CONURES 9
    2. TYPES OF CONURES TO CONSIDER 12
    3. CONURES CAN BE EASY TO FIND 13
    4. ONE CONURE OR TWO 14
    5. CONURE CAGES DON'T REQUIRE A LOT OF SPACE 16
CHAPTER THREE 18
    CARE & DIET REQUIREMENTS OF PET CONURES 18
    CONURE CARE 19
    CONURE DIET 20
CHAPTER FOUR 22
    DIFFERENT TYPES OF CONURES 22
    SUN CONURE (ARATINGA SOLSTITIALIS) 22

JENDAY CONURE (ARATINGA JANDAY)........25

NANDAY CONURE (NANDAYUS NENDAY).....26

BLUE CROWNED CONURE (THECTOCERCUS ACUTICAUDATA)..28

MAROON BELLIED CONURE (PYRRHURA FRONTALIS)...30

GREEN CHEEKED CONURE (PYRRHURA MOLINAE) 32

PEACH FRONTED CONURE (EUPSITTULA AUREA)..34

DUSKY HEADED CONURE (EUPSITTULA WEDDELLII) 37

RED MASKED CONURE (PSITTACARA ERYTHROGENYS)..39

PATAGONIAN CONURE (CYANOLISEUS PATAGONUS) 41

THE END 45

CHAPTER ONE

INTRODUCTION

Conure parrots, are pleasant little birds which might be colourful and full of individual. Hand reared conures make amazing pets and are extremely popular with bird fans all around the global. Some of the greater famous, and easily to be had varieties of conures kept as puppy birds, consist of the subsequent: Sun Conure, Jenday Conure, Nanday Conure, Blue Crowned Conure, Maroon Bellied Conure, Green Cheeked Conure, Peach Fronted Conure, Dusky

Headed Conure, Red Masked Conure, and the Patagonian Conure. Conures, which range in length from small to medium, frequently appeal human beings with their playfulness and inquisitive personalities. They usually want to be where the family hobby is, that may consist of mealtime and striking out with their preferred humans.

Conures have huge personalities for such small birds. They are smart and interactive, however also are extra vulnerable to behavioral issues than the greater not unusual, smaller cockatiels or budgies. Conures require devoted care takers who will paintings with them to manual their conduct." Below are a few guidelines.

THEY LOVE TO PLAY

They are very lively parrots that like to play, explore and chunk. Lots of toys are recommended to hold their beaks from "getting busy" in your furniture.

• Toys can also be matters that I wager you in no way idea were toys at all! Please talk over with the foraging page for smooth, less expensive or FREE suggestions to entertain your pet.

THEY ARE SMART

Most will keep their very own with any of the mid-sized or medium-large parrots in terms of smartness. They may be taught simple tricks pretty without difficulty and more complicated hints with some education.

CHAPTER TWO

REASONS CONURES MAKE GREAT FAMILY PETS

Families looking for a bird as a puppy chicken may additionally encounter conures while doing their studies. With extra than one hundred exceptional species and subspecies of conures, parents and youngsters can without difficulty be overwhelmed by way of all the conures they can choose from. Conures make extremely good family pets, in quick, because:

1. They adapt effortlessly.

2. There are many sorts of conures that are ideal for first or experienced chook owners.

3. Conures are fairly priced and easily obtainable. You can undertake too!

4. Conures are terrific in businesses or by myself.

5. Conures' cages don't take in as plenty space.

1. ADAPTABLE AND RESILIENT CONURES

Conures are "fairly bendy and [an] smooth going fowl," explains Cheryl Burns, aviculturist and previous president of the Interational Conure Association. Conures' adaptability allows them to regulate without difficulty to their new surroundings and own family's agenda. Burns said that conures are suitable at:

SCHEDULES FOR EATING

- Taking to own family members intuitively because they're certainly "playful and curious"

- Being boarded and shifting with a circle of relatives.

Jamie Whittaker of ABC Birds in Humble, Texas explains conures may be trained to, "are available and out of the cage, stay on their playstand, perform tricks, bow, visit other humans," alongside transferring onto someone's hand and may be educated to be groomed. Whittaker stated, "[conures] make suitable family pets due to the fact they are now not intimidating searching so children are inclined to deal with them."

2. TYPES OF CONURES TO CONSIDER

Whittaker recommends green-cheeked conures because they're quieter than the Aratinga conure species. Green-cheeked conures are available in colour mutations such as not unusual maroon tail and inexperienced body, cinnamon, turquoise and blue and yellow-sided. Similar in size to inexperienced-cheeked conures, about 10 inches in period, purple-bellied conures and black-capped conures are recommended by means of Whittaker due to the fact they're quieter than the Arantinga-kind conures. Other advocated conure species, consistent with Whittaker, encompass 1/2-moon conures, peach-fronted conures and dusky sub-species of the Arantinga-kind conures, because they are simplest barely louder than an inexperienced-cheeked conure.

3. CONURES CAN BE EASY TO FIND

Depending at the form of conure and wherein one is sold, prices range. Green-cheeked conures have a mean charge variety of

$149 to $350, according to Whittaker, with breeders probable cheaper and pet stores being more steeply-priced. You can also considering adopting a conure too!

4. ONE CONURE OR TWO

Whether a family wishes a unmarried conure or a couple of conures relies upon on the make-up and desire of the circle of relatives. Whittaker explains the variety of conures that might be suitable for a own family relies upon on a family's lifestyle, the number of humans that loves birds inside the domestic and the sociability of conures. As Whittaker explains, "[conures] socialize well with different birds; they socialize with other human beings," demonstrating how conures can live by myself or with one or multiple different conures, even to ten to 12 partner conures or greater because conures revel in the enterprise of other birds. This leaves discretion as much as the family's wishes and desires. Whether a circle of relatives desires a single conure or a couple of conures relies upon at the makeup and choice of the own family.

5. CONURE CAGES DON'T REQUIRE A LOT OF SPACE

Burns provides that conures, "don't absorb a number of space." Compared to a macaw cage, specially! Ranging from 8 to fourteen or 16 inches in period, which includes their tail, conures can move around a 24- to 36-inch hen cage without brushing up towards the perimeters. This doesn't suggest you can put the conure in a nook and forget about about him! Conures like to grasp outdoor of their cage, on their playstand or with you!

CHAPTER THREE

CARE & DIET REQUIREMENTS OF PET CONURES

Conure parrots, are pleasant little birds which can be colourful and full of character. Hand reared conures make extremely good pets and are extraordinarily famous with fowl enthusiasts everywhere in the global. Some of the more popular, and without problems available forms of conures saved as pet birds, encompass the subsequent: Sun Conure, Jenday Conure, Nanday Conure, Blue

Crowned Conure, Maroon Bellied Conure, Green Cheeked Conure, Peach Fronted Conure, Dusky Headed Conure, Red Masked Conure, and the Patagonian Conure.

CONURE CARE

Conures are energetic birds, and consequently conure chook cages need to be pretty big relative to body size, outfitted with lots of toys, specially matters to bite, and noisy toys like bells and rattles, to offer stimulation and prevent boredom. As they are sensible birds that like to have interaction and play, it is easy to train all forms of conures to carry out hints. They will without problems lie the wrong way up within the palm of your hand and play dead. They also love water, and it is encouraged that a chicken tub be furnished – rather a sprig bathe in warm weather will always be liked.

CONURE DIET

A balanced food regimen of entire grains, fruit, vegetables, seeds and nuts is usually recommended for all styles of conures to ensure that they continue to be in accurate fitness. Feed commercial seed and pellet mixes collectively with a spread of sparkling fruit and vegetables. Conures love apple, corn at the cob, sprouted seeds, in addition to a cooked blend of corn and peas, together with the mixes to be had for pigeons. Foods to keep away from encompass chocolate, alcohol, onions and avocado pear, which is pretty toxic to parrots.

CHAPTER FOUR

DIFFERENT TYPES OF CONURES

SUN CONURE (ARATINGA SOLSTITIALIS)

DESCRIPTION: The Sun Conure is a remarkably putting hen – with its splash of bold colorations it is honestly a stunning bird indeed. The frame of the Sun Conure is predominantly shiny yellow to orange, with darkish orange-crimson highlights around the cheeks and belly. The wings are yellow with inexperienced splashes throughout and iridescent blue feathers at the wing tips. The tail is inexperienced and blue.

- Size: 12 inches
- Weight: 100-130 grams
- Lifespan: 25-30 years
- Minimum Cage Size: 24 x 24 x 36 inches

CHARACTERISTICS: The Sun Conure is a tremendously sociable, and affectionate hen. It is lively, fun-loving, and acrobatic, making a very playful pet so as to conveniently learn to carry out tricks. It is extremely vocal, and is also very alert and an great watchdog; screeching loudly to bring in the advent of a person at the door, or to welcome its proprietor domestic after a hard days paintings.

Sun conures are very worrying, requiring masses of attention and human interaction. They are ranked as one of the noisiest types of conures, and are therefore no longer recommended for apartment dwellers, or proprietors with a low tolerance level to noise. However, if you can positioned up with their screeching, they have got beauty, brains, are large in character and make super pets.

JENDAY CONURE (ARATINGA JANDAY)

DESCRIPTION: The Jenday Conure is very much like the Sun Conure in both seems and persona. While it is comparable in colour to the Sun Conure, the color is in distinct bands instead of splashes of colour throughout. The head is a solid yellow, the top frame and wings are vibrant inexperienced, even as the stomach is shiny orange-crimson. The tail is green and blue.

- Size: 12 inches

- Weight: 100-130 grams

- Lifespan: 25-30 years

- Minimum Cage Size: 24 x 24 x 36 inches.

Characteristics: Similar to the sun conure.

NANDAY CONURE (NANDAYUS NENDAY)

DESCRIPTION: The Nanday Conure is a little dull while in comparison to the coloring of the Sun Conure and Jenday Conure, however he has a massive persona to make up for this. The Nanday Conure has a black head, inexperienced body and wings with blue number one flight and tail feathers. It has a touch of vivid pink on the legs.

- Size: 13 inches

- Weight: 135-145 grams

- Lifespan: 25-30 years

- Minimum Cage Size: 24 x 24 x 48 inches.

CHARACTERISTICS: Nanday Conures make extraordinary pets, but as they may be also willing to be very noisy and negative; they're no longer appropriate for rental living.

BLUE CROWNED CONURE (THECTOCERCUS ACUTICAUDATA)

DESCRIPTION: The Blue Crowned Conure (or Sharp Tailed Conure) is predominantly inexperienced all over the body, however because the call shows, it has a blue crown on the pinnacle which includes shades of blue. The underside of the tail is a color of red starting from red to darkish rust in shade.

- Size: 15 inches

- Weight: 115-130 grams

- Lifespan: 25-30 years

- Minimum Cage Size: 24 x 24 x 48 inches

CHARACTERISTICS: The Blue Crowned Conure is a smart, candy natured, playful hen to be able to effortlessly examine hints, and additionally make very good talkers. They also have a tendency to be as an alternative noisy and destructive, in order that they need masses of toys to chew and aren't appropriate for rental dwelling.

MAROON BELLIED CONURE (PYRRHURA FRONTALIS)

DESCRIPTION: The Maroon Bellied Conure is a small conure, predominantly inexperienced in colour, with a yellowish-inexperienced barred breast and facets. It has a maroon belly, the primary wing feathers are blue-green in shade, and the tail is inexperienced on top and light maroon below. It has a mild brown patch masking the ears.

- Size: 10 inches

- Weight: 65-85 grams

- Lifespan: two decades

Minimum Cage Size: 20 x 20 x 30 inches with 1/2-5/8 inch bar spacing

CHARACTERISTICS: Maroon Bellied Conures are extraordinarily social, clever, affectionate, playful and like to engage. While they have got a shrill call, they are taken into consideration one of the quieter types of conures, and do not screech to the equal diploma as their large cousins. They aren't top talkers.

GREEN CHEEKED CONURE (PYRRHURA MOLINAE)

DESCRIPTION: Very similar in seems and nature to the Maroon Bellied Conure, the Green Cheeks are in most cases green at the frame, with gray breasts, maroon tails and blue number one flight feathers. The top of the head is a darker shade of gray and the cheeks are green. Mutations in are commonplace in captivity, and captive breeding has produced the subsequent coloration variations in

Green Cheek Conures: Cinnamon, Turquoise and Yellow Sided Green Cheeks, as well as Suncheek, and Pineapple Conures.

- Size: 10 inches

- Weight: 65-85 grams

- Lifespan: 15 years

- Minimum Cage Size: 20 x 20 x 30 inches with 1/2-5/8 inch bar spacing

Characteristics: These feisty little birds are complete of amusing, candy natured, friendly, and just love interest. They are relatively social and do nicely in communal aviaries. By conure standards, they're fairly quiet, and provide a shrill whistle or natter away rather than screech, making them greater appropriate for people with touchy hearing and for condominium dwellers.

Special Notes: Endangered in the wild, indexed on CITES II

PEACH FRONTED CONURE (EUPSITTULA AUREA)

DESCRIPTION: The Peach Fronted Conure has a green top body, with a gray-inexperienced breast and lighter lime green coloring at the belly. The brow and centre of the crown are brilliant orange with blue on the perimeters of the crown surrounding the eyes. The rest of the pinnacle is inexperienced. The tail is inexperienced with blue suggestions, and the wings green with black recommendations. The black beak of the Peach Fronted Conure distinguish it from the Orange Fronted and Half Moon conures.

- Size: 10 inches

- Weight: 105 grams

- Lifespan: 25-30 years

- Minimum Cage Size: 24 x 24 x 36 inches

CHARACTERISTICS: The Peach Fronted Conure has a sweet disposition, it's far cuddly and playful via nature, and makes a lovable puppy. As they are rather quiet by conure requirements, they may be perfect for condominium dwellers or the ones no longer keen on the raucous nature of different varieties of conures.

DUSKY HEADED CONURE (EUPSITTULA WEDDELLII)

DESCRIPTION: The Dusky Headed Conure is alternatively stupid in color, predominantly inexperienced all over, with yellow inexperienced stomach and a grey-brown head. The number one flight feathers are black edged with blue, and the tail is blue on top and black below.

- Size: 11-12 inches

- Weight: 91-115 grams

- Lifespan: 30+ years

- Minimum Cage Size: 36 x 24 x 30 inches

CHARACTERISTICS: While Dusky Headed Conures are not as striking as some of the alternative kinds of conures, they may be additionally not as traumatic. They are fairly quiet as conures go, and are sweet natured, and for that reason make excellent pets for children.

RED MASKED CONURE (PSITTACARA ERYTHROGENYS)

DESCRIPTION: The Red Masked Conure (or Cherry Headed Conure) is shiny green at the body, with lighter green on the breast. The head is a bold pink, at the same time as the attention ring is a fundamental white. They have purple splashes on the wings inside the vicinity of the shoulder. Immature birds are completely inexperienced and most effective acquire their pink coloring at round six months old.

- Size: 13 inches

- Weight: 200 grams

- Lifespan: 30+ years

- Minimum Cage Size: 24 x 24 x 48 inches

CHARACTERISTICS: Red Masked Conures are one in all the bigger forms of conures. They are very playful, active birds that make properly pets. Red Masked conures are very vocal, and can be as a substitute noisy at times, but as they are properly mimics, you can effortlessly educate them to talk.

PATAGONIAN CONURE (CYANOLISEUS PATAGONUS)

DESCRIPTION: The Patagonian Conure is the biggest species of conure, achieving up to 20 inches from head to tail. It is predominantly darkish olive green-brown in coloration, with a gray breast, a orange-purple stomach patch edged with yellow, and crimson at the legs. It has a white collar around the neck, and the number one flight feathers are blue.

- Size: 17-20 inches

- Weight: 300-450 grams

- Lifespan: 20-30 years

- Minimum Cage Size: 30 x 36 x 36 inches

CHARACTERISTICS: Like all kinds of conures, the Patagonian makes a superb cuddly pet, that loves to play. They are very vocal, and at the same time as they may be quite noisy, they also make properly talkers. Their huge size makes them the best desire for a person who's drawn to conures, however who would opt for a larger size chook as a pet.

There are many different kinds of conures to be had at the puppy marketplace, they come in a selection of sizes and hues, and vary to some extent in their vocal ability. Some are especially demure and quiet, at the same time as others are extremely raucous and vocal, and this desires to be considered whilst choosing a conure to fit your way of life.

Conures are extraordinarily social birds, that is why hand-raised conures make such properly pets. However, because of their social nature, they require plenty of interest and human interaction. If they do now not get hold of this they could come to be very noisy in their efforts to attract interest. If you do no longer have the time to commit to those endearing birds, then it's miles advocated which you alternatively get a much less annoying pet, as it would no longer be honest to the hen – or your neighbors – if you cannot supply them the attention they deserve.

THE END

Printed in Great Britain
by Amazon